Disney VILLAINS Cookbook

RECIPES
Joy Howard, with additional recipes by Deanna F. Cook
and Cynthia Littlefield

PHOTOGRAPHY
Joe St. Pierre

FOOD STYLING
Joy Howard

ILLUSTRATIONS
The Disney Storybook Art Team

DESIGN
Megan Youngquist

Published by Disney Press, an imprint of Buena Vista Books, Inc.
No part of this book may be reproduced or transmitted in any form or by any means,
electronic or mechanical, including photocopying, recording,
or by any information storage and retrieval system, without written permission from the publisher.
For information address Disney Press, 1200 Grand Central Avenue,
Glendale, California 91201.

Printed in the United States of America
First Hardcover Edition, July 2023
1 3 5 7 9 10 8 6 4 2
Library of Congress Control Number: 2022945606
FAC-034274-23138
ISBN 978-1-368-07498-8
Visit www.disneybooks.com

DISNEY VILLAINS Cookbook

DISNEY PRESS

Los Angeles • New York

Contents

Basics

No one makes mischief quite like a Disney Villain! Whether it's the Queen's poison apple or Yzma's shape-shifting potions, Ursula's bubbling undersea cauldron full of spells or King Candy's deceptively delicious domain in *Sugar Rush*, the villains know how to wreak havoc—especially by creating mysterious concoctions. Perhaps aspiring chefs can learn a thing or two from their skillful brewing . . . but cooking doesn't have to be villainous! This cookbook is your guide to using the villains' secrets to create scrumptious confections that will satisfy even the muscular Gaston's appetite.

Turn the page to discover fifty villain-inspired recipes—from breakfast, lunch, and dinner, to beverages, sides, snacks, and desserts. The recipes are rated on a five 🍎 scale, so if you're a beginner, don't worry! Start with an easier dish { 🍎 } and work your way up to the more complicated recipes { 🍎 🍎 🍎 🍎 🍎 }.

Now put on your best villainous disguise and get ready to make some delicious treats that are so wickedly good, they might just cast some magic on you!

Before You Begin

Cooking is a lot of fun, but before you get started, there are some important things to remember. Always, always ask a parent for permission. Even the villains need help from their trusty sidekicks to brew their concoctions successfully. If you need to use a stove, oven, blender, or mixer for a recipe, make sure to ask an adult to help you. Here are a few other tips to keep in mind.

- If you have long hair, tie it back. You don't want it to end up in the food or near a hot stove.

- Make sure your clothing isn't loose enough to touch a stovetop burner. If you're wearing long sleeves, push them up to your elbows.

- Put on an apron to keep your outfit from getting stained.

- Wash your hands with water and soap for at least twenty seconds so they will be clean when you handle the ingredients.

- Take a few minutes to read the whole recipe so that nothing will come as a surprise once you get started.

- Gather all the equipment you'll need, such as measuring spoons, bowls, baking pans, and utensils, before you get out the ingredients.

Measuring Ingredients

To make sure a recipe turns out just the way it's supposed to, you need to measure ingredients exactly. Here are some helpful hints and tips.

- For liquids like milk, water, or oil, use a measuring cup with a spout designed for pouring.

- A dry ingredient, such as flour, sugar, or cocoa, should be spooned into a measuring cup without a spout. Then, to check that you have the exact amount, scrape the flat edge of a butter knife across the rim of the cup to remove any extra.

- A chunky ingredient should be spooned into a measuring cup and then patted gently, just enough to even out the top without packing it down. Shredded ingredients are also measured this way.

- Brown sugar should be packed into a measuring cup to press out any air bubbles.

- Measuring butter is really easy if you use sticks that have tablespoon marks printed on the wrapper. All you have to do is slice the butter where the line is.

Safety First!

Even when they're getting up to a little villainy, a good cook never forgets that safety always comes first in the kitchen. Here are some important rules to follow.

Using knives, peelers, graters, and small kitchen appliances

- Never use a kitchen appliance or sharp utensil without asking an adult for help.

- Always use a cutting board when slicing or chopping ingredients. Grip the knife handle firmly, holding it so that the sharp edge is facing downward. Then slice through the ingredient, moving the knife away from yourself.

- After slicing raw meat or fish, wash the knife (with an adult's help) as well as the cutting board. You should also wash your hands with water and soap for at least twenty seconds before working with other ingredients.

- If you drop a knife, don't try to catch it. Instead, quickly step back and let the knife fall to the countertop or floor before picking it up by the handle.

- When using a vegetable peeler, press the edge of the blade into the vegetable's skin and then push the peeler away from yourself. Keep in mind that the more pressure you use, the thicker the peeling will be.

- Use electrical appliances, such as mixers and blenders, in a cleared space far away from the sink and other wet areas. And always unplug a mixer or blender before scraping a mixture from the beaters or blades.

Working around hot things

- Always ask an adult for help around a hot stovetop or oven.

- Make sure to point the handle of a stovetop pan away from you so you won't knock into it and accidentally tip the pot over.

- Use pot holders every time you touch a stovetop pot or skillet—even if it's just the lid. You should also use pot holders whenever you put a pan in the oven or take it out.

- Remember, steam can burn! Be sure to step back a bit when straining hot foods, such as pasta or cooked vegetables.

- Don't forget to shut off the oven or stove burner when the food is done baking or cooking.

Preparing Fruits and Vegetables

It's important to wash produce before adding it to a recipe. Here are some tips for making sure fruits and vegetables are clean and ready to use.

- Rinse produce well under plain running water. Don't use soap! If the produce is firm, like an apple or carrot, rub the surface to help remove any garden soil or grit. You can put softer fruits and vegetables, such as berries and broccoli florets, in a small colander or strainer before rinsing.

- Use a vegetable brush to scrub vegetables that grow underground, like potatoes and carrots. You should also scrub any fruits and vegetables that grow right on the ground, such as cucumbers and melons.

- Dry washed produce with a paper towel or reusable cleaning cloth and cut off any bruised parts before using it in a recipe.

Cleaning Up

A good cook always leaves the kitchen as tidy as they found it. This means cleaning all the bowls, pots, pans, and utensils you used to prepare the recipe. Here are some tips for making sure everything is spick-and-span.

- Always ask an adult for help washing knives and appliances with sharp blades, such as a blender or food processor.

- As you cook, try to give each bowl and utensil a quick rinse as soon as you're done with it. That way leftover food or batter won't stick to it before you can wash it with soap and water.

- Put all the ingredients back where they belong so you'll know just where to find them the next time you cook.

- Wipe down your work area—including the countertop and sink—with a damp paper towel or reusable cleaning cloth.

- Double-check that all the appliances you used are turned off before you leave the kitchen.

- Hang up your apron, or put it in the laundry if it needs to be washed.

Breakfast

Ingredients

½ cup apple juice

1 frozen banana

1 cup frozen mango

4 ice cubes

Toppings

sliced strawberries
and blueberries

half an apple

Tip

*If you'd prefer, you can
slice up the apple at
the center of the smoothie
to make it easier
to eat—or try another
fruity topping!*

The Queen's Bewitching Apple Bowl

The Queen is quite the expert when it comes to apples!
This simple smoothie bowl recipe will have you making
your own magic with apples in no time.

Directions

1. Ask an adult for help with the blender. Place the apple juice,
   frozen banana, frozen mango, and ice cubes into the blender.

2. Blend the ingredients until they are smooth and creamy.

3. Pour the smoothie into a bowl, add your preferred toppings,
   and serve with a spoon.

Spotted Scones

The fashion-obsessed Cruella is best known for her fixation on fabulous spotted clothes, but she'd likely devour a batch of these polka-dot delights, too. They're flavored with orange zest and chocolate chips, and topped with sparkling sugar.

Directions

1. Line a baking sheet with parchment paper. In a large bowl, whisk together the flour, sugar, salt, baking powder, orange zest, and chocolate chips. With an adult's help, use a box grater to grate the butter into the flour mixture. Use your hands to toss the butter into the flour a few times.

2. In another bowl, whisk together 1 egg, the vanilla, and the half-and-half. Combine the two mixtures and blend until the flour is moistened. Do not overmix.

3. Turn the dough out onto a lightly floured surface. Pat it into a ½-inch-thick circle and cut into 8 even wedges. Place the scones on the prepared baking sheet, then refrigerate while the oven heats.

4. Ask an adult for help with the oven. Heat the oven to 400°F. Whisk together the remaining egg with 1 tablespoon water. Brush the top of each scone with the egg wash and sprinkle generously with coarse sugar. Bake the scones until golden brown on the top and bottom, about 20 minutes, rotating the pan halfway through.

Makes 8

Ingredients

2 cups flour, plus more for dusting

3 Tbsp sugar

½ tsp kosher salt

2 tsp baking powder

¾ tsp orange zest

½ cup semisweet chocolate chips

½ cup (1 stick) cold unsalted butter

2 eggs

1¼ tsp vanilla extract

½ cup half-and-half

Coarse sparkling sugar

Tip

You can find sparkling sugar at some grocery stores and most craft stores in the baking section.

Ingredients

1 (14-inch) demi
baguette

4 eggs

3 Tbsp heavy cream

¼ tsp kosher salt

Black pepper

⅓ cup shredded cheddar

1 scallion, chopped

2 strips cooked bacon,
roughly chopped

Tip

*Check out page 130
for a step-by-step guide
on how to trim the
baguette so you can fill
it with the egg mixture.*

Baguette Breakfast Beaks

This dish, featuring eggs baked right into a loaf of toasty
bread, is sliced into wedges shaped like a bird's beak as a nod
to the winged accomplices Iago and the Raven. Perch them on
a plate for your next weekend brunch and watch every slice
fly away!

Directions

1. Ask an adult for help with the oven. Heat the oven to 350°F.
   Have an adult use a sharp knife to cut a rectangle out of the
   baguette, being careful not to cut through the sides or bottom.
   Place the loaf on a baking sheet.

2. In a large liquid measuring
   cup, whisk together the eggs,
   heavy cream, salt, and a few
   grinds of pepper. Stir in the
   cheddar, scallion, and bacon.
   Carefully pour the mixture into
   the baguette (you may have
   a little left over).

3. Bake until the egg is
   puffy and set, about 25
   minutes. Let sit 5 minutes,
   then slice into 8 even
   wedges. Serve immediately.

Rosy Red Oatmeal

The cantankerous Queen of Hearts is not easy to please, though given her affinity for red, she might approve of a breakfast like this rose-tinted bowl. Fresh strawberries give the bowl its blushing hue and are also sliced, shaped into hearts, and scattered on top.

Directions

1. In a blender, pulse the milk and strawberries until the berries are in small chunks.

2. Ask an adult for help at the stove. Place the mixture in a medium saucepan. Bring to a boil.

3. Add the oats and a pinch of salt. Reduce the heat to low and cook until done, about 5 minutes. Add the maple syrup. Let cool slightly.

4. While the oatmeal cools, slice each remaining berry. Trim the tops of each slice to form a heart shape. Evenly divide the oatmeal between two bowls, then top each portion with strawberry hearts. Serve immediately.

Serves 2

Ingredients

1½ cups oat milk

1½ cups strawberries, trimmed and halved, plus 2 more for slicing

1 cup quick oats

Kosher salt

2 Tbsp maple syrup

Tip

Make this oatmeal your own by experimenting with other toppings like nuts, fruit, and more.

Ingredients

12 large eggs

½ cup heavy cream

¾ tsp kosher salt

½ tsp black pepper

1 Tbsp olive oil

4 oz cremini mushrooms, sliced

2 scallions, sliced, whites and greens separated

2 cups fresh baby spinach, roughly chopped

1½ cups shredded cheddar

Tip

Once you learn how to make the frittata base, you can play around with what types of cheese, veggies, or other toppings to add to the mix!

Dozen-Egg Frittata

Gaston claims to eat five dozen eggs a day to maintain his muscular figure. You need only one dozen eggs to make this dish, but there will still be plenty for a crowd. An added bonus: there's spinach, mushrooms, and cheddar tucked into every bite.

Directions

1. Ask an adult for help with the oven. Heat the oven to 400°F. In a medium bowl, whisk together the eggs, heavy cream, salt, and pepper. Set aside.

2. Ask an adult for help at the stove. In a 9- or 10-inch cast-iron skillet over medium heat, warm the oil. Add the mushrooms and scallion whites and cook until the mushrooms and scallions have softened, about 5 minutes. Stir in the spinach and scallion greens and cook until wilted, about 2 minutes.

3. Set aside a few tablespoons of the cheese. Add the egg mixture and remaining cheese to the skillet and stir to combine. Top with the reserved cheese.

4. Reduce the heat to medium low and continue to cook undisturbed until beginning to set around the edges, about 5 minutes. With an adult's help, place the skillet in the oven and bake until set, about 10 to 15 minutes more. Let cool a few minutes before slicing and serving.

Blackberry French Toast Casserole

Dark berries and spices conjure a wickedly tasty breakfast that rivals any spell Maleficent could cast. Letting this dish rest for a while after it comes out of the oven gives it more time to set and makes it even more delicious.

Directions

1. Ask an adult for help with the oven. Heat the oven to 325°F. Spread the bread on a baking sheet and bake until dried out but not browned, about 15 minutes, turning halfway through. Let cool on the pan, then transfer to a large bowl.

2. Butter an 8-inch baking dish. In a medium bowl, whisk together the egg yolks and sugar. Add the half-and-half, vanilla, salt, cinnamon, and nutmeg and whisk until evenly blended. Pour the mixture over the bread and gently toss to evenly moisten the bread.

3. Cover the bottom of the baking dish with half the bread cubes. Sprinkle on half the berries. Repeat with the other halves of the bread cubes and berries. Pour any remaining egg mixture over the bread and berries, cover the casserole, and refrigerate 30 minutes.

4. Bake the dish until the casserole is set in the center, about 1 hour, rotating the pan halfway through. Let the casserole rest at least 15 minutes and dust with confectioners' sugar, if using, before serving.

Serves 9

Ingredients

¾ loaf challah bread, diced into 1-inch cubes (8 cups)

Butter, for greasing

4 egg yolks

½ cup sugar

3 cups half-and-half

1¾ tsp vanilla extract

¼ tsp kosher salt

1¼ tsp ground cinnamon

¼ tsp ground nutmeg

2 cups blackberries

Confectioners' sugar, for dusting (optional)

Tip

Not sure how to separate egg yolks from the rest of the egg? **Check out the Glossary on page 140!**

Lunch

Kronk's Spinach Puffs

Yzma's faithful sidekick, Kronk, is a talented chef, and spinach puffs are one of his specialties. Make this recipe your own "new groove"!

Directions

1. Ask an adult for help with the oven. Heat the oven to 400°F. Use a mesh colander or cheesecloth to squeeze and drain the water from the spinach. Place in a medium bowl with the scallions, feta, cottage cheese, Parmesan, 2 eggs, and salt and pepper. Stir to combine.

2. Ask an adult for help with knives. Evenly cut each pastry sheet into 9 squares. Press each dough portion into the well of a standard cupcake pan, letting the corners hang over the edges. Spoon a generous tablespoon of the spinach mixture into each pastry.

3. Gather the corners of each dough square and pinch them closed. In a small bowl, whisk together the remaining egg with 1 tablespoon water. Brush the tops of the pastries with this egg wash. Bake until golden and crisp, about 25 minutes. Let cool slightly before serving.

Makes 9

Ingredients

1 pound frozen spinach, thawed and squeezed

4 scallions, chopped

⅓ cup crumbled feta

⅓ cup cottage cheese

2 Tbsp shredded Parmesan

3 eggs

¾ tsp kosher salt

⅛ tsp white pepper

2 sheets frozen puff pastry from a 17-oz package, thawed

Tip

If you use the microwave or stovetop to thaw your spinach, be sure to let the spinach cool completely. Using it while still hot could cause the eggs to start cooking too quickly.

Makes 8

Ingredients

2½ cups chopped
rotisserie chicken

⅓ cup mayonnaise

2 Tbsp chopped roasted
red bell pepper

1 large stalk celery, sliced

1 Tbsp chopped chives,
plus more for garnish

¼ cup chopped smoked
almonds

¼ tsp smoked paprika,
plus more for garnish

Black pepper

1 small head Bibb lettuce

Tip

*As an alternative to
using a sharp knife, you
can snip the celery,
bell pepper, and chives
with kitchen shears.*

Smoky Chicken Salad Cups

Hades, the god of the Underworld, is known for his ability to create flames. While not as fiery as some of his creations, this chicken salad still has a bit of smolder: both the almonds and paprika are the smoked variety, which gives the lettuce cups a unique flavor.

Directions

1. In a large bowl, stir together the chicken, mayonnaise, bell pepper, celery, chives, almonds, and paprika. Season lightly with black pepper, then taste, and adjust seasoning if needed.

2. Tear 8 leaves from the head of lettuce. Fill each with ⅓ cup of the salad. Serve immediately.

Mini Tamatoa Seaweed Rolls

A batch of these hand rolls will attract hungry friends, just as Tamatoa's shiny shell draws in curious fish. Ask an adult to help you prep the vegetables, and don't worry too much about the look of the end result. It will be tasty no matter what!

Directions

1. Cook the rice according to the package directions.

2. Meanwhile, in a small bowl, stir together the vinegar, sugar, and salt until the latter two are dissolved. Pour the mixture over the rice, add the sesame seeds, and stir to coat evenly. Let the rice mixture cool completely.

3. Spread a heaping ¼ cup of rice on a nori sheet. Arrange one-eighth of the carrot, cucumber, and avocado in the center of the sheet (vegetables can be trimmed if they are too long). Roll into a cone or log, as shown (see page 131). Repeat with the remaining nori, rice, and vegetables. Serve immediately with soy sauce.

Makes 8

Ingredients

¾ cup uncooked sushi rice

2 Tbsp rice vinegar

1½ tsp sugar

¼ tsp kosher salt

1 tsp black sesame seeds

4 large sheets nori, halved crosswise

1 large carrot, cut into matchsticks

1–2 Persian cucumbers, cut into matchsticks

1 large avocado, sliced

Soy sauce, for dipping

Tip

Check out page 131 for a step-by-step guide on how to create these seaweed rolls!

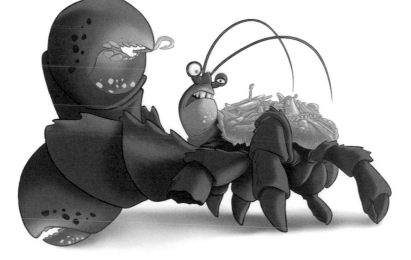

Ingredients

Flour, for dusting

1 (9-inch) refrigerated piecrust

2 Tbsp pizza sauce

10 pepperoni slices, roughly chopped

½ cup shredded mozzarella

1 large egg

12 black olives

Tip

It's tempting to stack these pockets extra high with fillings, but try to use filling sparingly. Using less will make it easier to form the all-important lion's mane.

Roaring Pizza Pockets

Want to take "pride" in your lunch? Try making these Scar-shaped pockets that combine the delicious flavors of pepperoni pizza with buttery pie crust.

Directions

1. Ask an adult for help with the oven. Heat the oven to 400°F and line a baking sheet with parchment paper. On a lightly floured surface, roll out the piecrust to a 13-inch circle. Use a 2½-inch round cutter to shape 12 circles from the dough, gathering and rerolling the dough as needed.

2. Arrange half the dough rounds on the prepared baking sheet. Top each with 1 teaspoon sauce, leaving a 1-inch border. Add ⅙ of the chopped pepperoni slices and a heaping tablespoon mozzarella to each. (You will have some cheese left over.)

3. Whisk the egg in a small bowl with 1 tablespoon water. Brush the edges of each filling-topped dough round with the egg wash, then top each with one of the remaining dough rounds. Use a fork to crimp the edges of each pocket, then brush their tops with the egg wash. Trim the olives into 12 eyes and 6 noses. Add a set to each pocket, then add cheese whiskers, as shown.

4. Bake the pockets until golden brown, about 15 minutes. Serve immediately.

Playing-Card Sandwiches

These teensy sandwiches filled with hummus and cucumber are suited just like the Queen of Hearts' loyal playing-card soldiers. But you can change up what's inside each bite any way you wish (just as the Queen would surely do!). Switch up the vegetables or sandwich spread, or swap them both for cream cheese and jelly.

Directions

1. Spread one side of each bread slice with the hummus. Arrange the cucumbers on half the bread slices, then top each with a remaining slice, hummus side down.

2. Use mini diamond, heart, club, and spade cookie cutters to cut small shapes from each sandwich. Discard the scraps and serve.

Makes 8

Ingredients

4 slices of your favorite sandwich bread

6 Tbsp hummus

12 thin slices cucumber

Tip

Be sure to slice the cucumber extra thin so it will be easier to cut through with the cookie cutters.

Serves about 10

Ingredients

1 Tbsp olive oil

1 Tbsp butter

1 large onion

2 medium carrots, chopped

2 stalks celery, chopped

2 garlic cloves, minced

1 tsp grated fresh ginger

½ tsp ground cumin

1 tsp kosher salt

½ tsp black pepper

2 lb (about 6 cups) butternut squash, chopped

2 medium apples, peeled and chopped

4 cups chicken broth

Tip

Enjoy this soup topped with croutons or with a slice of bread for sopping up the last drop.

Golden Squash and Apple Soup

The Queen used an apple to cast a spell, but the fruit in this recipe supplies nothing more than a touch of sweetness to an already yummy golden soup.

Directions

1. Ask an adult for help at the stove. In a large pot over medium heat, melt the oil and butter. Add the onion, carrots, and celery, and cook until softened, about 8 minutes. Add the garlic, ginger, cumin, salt, and pepper and cook 1 minute. Stir in the squash and apples, then add the broth.

2. Bring the mixture to a boil. Once boiling, reduce to a simmer, then let cook until the vegetables are completely softened, about 12 minutes.

3. With an adult's help, use a blender to puree the soup in batches—be careful; the soup will be very hot! Serve immediately.

Lady Tremaine's Emerald Grain Bowl

Lady Tremaine isn't known for her kindness, but this grain bowl made with vegetables and brown rice is as wholesome as can be. The broccoli, green beans, cucumbers, edamame, and herby avocado dressing in the bowl resemble Lady Tremaine's emerald green jewels.

Directions

1. Ask an adult for help with the oven. Heat the oven to 450°F. On a large sheet pan, toss the green beans and broccoli with the olive oil. Roast until slightly charred and tender, about 12 minutes. Season with salt and pepper to taste.

2. While the vegetables cook, make the dressing. Use a blender to puree the avocado, garlic, lime juice, cilantro, honey, and 3 tablespoons water until smooth. Season with salt and pepper to taste and blend once more.

3. Fill a bowl with one-quarter of the rice, then top with one-quarter each of the green bean and broccoli mixture, edamame, and cucumber. Top with a spoonful of the dressing. Serve immediately.

Serves 4

Ingredients

8 oz green beans

1 medium crown broccoli

1 Tbsp olive oil

Kosher salt

Black pepper

1 avocado, roughly chopped

1 garlic clove, grated

2 Tbsp lime juice

½ cup packed fresh cilantro

2 tsp honey

2 cups cooked brown rice, warmed

½ cup frozen edamame, thawed

2 Persian cucumbers, sliced

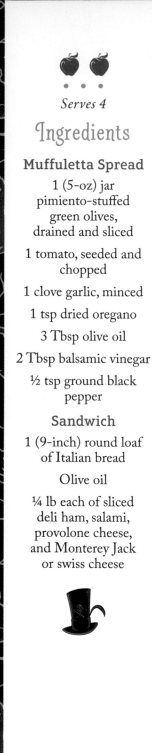

Serves 4

Ingredients

Muffuletta Spread

1 (5-oz) jar pimiento-stuffed green olives, drained and sliced

1 tomato, seeded and chopped

1 clove garlic, minced

1 tsp dried oregano

3 Tbsp olive oil

2 Tbsp balsamic vinegar

½ tsp ground black pepper

Sandwich

1 (9-inch) round loaf of Italian bread

Olive oil

¼ lb each of sliced deli ham, salami, provolone cheese, and Monterey Jack or swiss cheese

Muffuletta Sandwich

Dr. Facilier makes his mischief in the city of New Orleans, where this popular sandwich is all the rage.

Directions

1. Combine all the muffuletta spread ingredients in a bowl and stir until well mixed.

2. Slice the bread loaf in half lengthwise. Brush or drizzle the bottom piece with olive oil.

3. Layer on the meats, the cheeses, and the muffuletta spread, and then cover everything with the top half of the bread loaf.

4. Slice the sandwich into four wedges.

Dinner

Captain Hook's Stuffed Shells

After weeks of humble grub while out at sea, Captain Hook and his crew would no doubt appreciate a warm plate of this ocean-themed dish. Each oversized shell is stuffed with a pillowy dollop of ricotta and drenched in a delicious ladling of red sauce.

Ingredients

15 jumbo pasta shells

1 large egg

1¼ cups whole milk ricotta

1 garlic clove, grated

1 Tbsp fresh chopped parsley, plus more for garnish

¾ cup grated mozzarella

2 Tbsp grated Parmesan

½ tsp kosher salt

¼ tsp black pepper

1¼ cups marinara sauce

Directions

1. Ask an adult for help with the oven and stovetop. Heat the oven to 375°F and bring a large pot of water to a boil. Add the pasta to the water and cook according to the package directions.

2. While the pasta cooks, stir together the egg, ricotta, garlic, parsley, ½ cup mozzarella, 1 tablespoon Parmesan, salt, and pepper in a medium bowl.

3. Evenly spread ½ cup of the marinara over the bottom of an 8-inch baking dish. Add a spoonful of the ricotta mixture to the center of a pasta shell. Place the shell in the prepared baking dish. Repeat with the remaining shells and ricotta mixture.

4. Cover the shells with the remaining ¾ cup marinara and sprinkle on the remaining cheese. Cover the dish with foil and bake 30 minutes. Uncover the dish and bake 10 minutes more. Let sit for 5 to 10 minutes before serving.

Tip

*Pair this dish with a vegetable side—like Yzma's Roasted Broccoli with Parmesan on **page 66**.*

Ingredients

1 cup plain yogurt

2 tsp ground cumin

2 tsp smoked paprika

½ tsp ground
coriander

1 tsp lemon zest

2 garlic cloves, grated

1½ lb chicken breast,
cut into 1-inch cubes

1 large green bell pepper,
cut into large pieces

1 large yellow bell pepper,
cut into large pieces

1 large red onion,
cut into large pieces

Tip

*Do you know the
difference between
broiling and baking?*
**Check out the Glossary
on page 139** *to
find out.*

Spiced Chicken Kebabs

A marinade of yogurt, spices, and lots of lemon and garlic
gives these oven-broiled chicken skewers their unique taste.
It's a simple dish you can dress up by serving it on a fancy
platter—a choice the discerning Jafar would most certainly
approve of.

Directions

1. In a small bowl, stir together yogurt, cumin, paprika, coriander,
    lemon zest, and garlic. Set aside. Line a baking sheet with foil.

2. Ask an adult for help preparing the skewers. Thread the
    chicken, bell peppers, and onion onto eight 8-inch skewers in
    an alternating pattern. Place them on the prepared baking
    sheet.

3. Brush the skewers on all sides with the yogurt mixture.
    Place the pan in the refrigerator and let marinate at least
    1 hour.

4. Ask an adult for help with
    the oven. Heat the oven to
    425°F. Bake the skewers
    15 minutes. Remove from
    the oven, flip, and set the
    broiler to high. Broil the
    skewers until the chicken
    is cooked through and the
    vegetables are lightly
    charred around the edges,
    about 10 minutes. Serve
    immediately.

Shape-Shifting Pesto Pasta

If Hades's loyal minions Panic and Pain were to morph into a delicious bowl of pasta, it would probably look a lot like this one with its noodles in many shapes. A bright homemade basil pesto, Italian sausage, and fresh tomatoes round out the recipe.

Directions

1. Ask an adult for help at the stove. Warm a skillet over medium heat. Add 1 tablespoon oil and heat. Add the sausage and cook, stirring occasionally, until browned. Transfer to a paper-towel-lined plate.

2. Bring a large pot of water to a boil. Add the pasta and cook according to the package directions. Drain, reserving ¼ cup of the pasta water.

3. Meanwhile, in a blender or food processor, combine the basil, garlic, pine nuts, Parmesan, salt, and a few grinds of pepper. Pulse to chop. With the machine running, add the remaining oil in a slow, steady stream until well blended.

4. In a large bowl, toss together the cooked pasta, sausage, pesto, 2 tablespoons pasta water, and tomatoes. Add 1 or 2 tablespoons more of the pasta water if the pasta is dry. Serve immediately.

Serves 6

Ingredients

½ cup plus 1 Tbsp olive oil

12 oz Italian sausage

¾ lb mixed pasta (such as fusilli, rotelle, and rigatoni)

3 cups basil leaves

2 small garlic cloves, roughly chopped

3 Tbsp pine nuts

5 Tbsp Parmesan

1 tsp kosher salt

Black pepper

1 cup cherry tomatoes, halved

Tip

This dish is a clever way to use up small amounts of leftover dry pasta. Just be sure the cooking times are similar when you mix and match different shapes.

Ingredients

2 Tbsp vegetable oil

1 small garlic clove, grated

1 tsp grated fresh ginger

1 tsp garam masala

¾ tsp ground cumin

¼ tsp ground turmeric

¾ tsp kosher salt

¼ tsp black pepper

1 small onion, finely chopped

1 small head cauliflower, cut into florets

2 medium yellow potatoes, diced

3 whole plum tomatoes (from a 14-oz can)

¼ cup chopped cilantro

Tip

Enjoy this dish alongside a serving of naan or basmati rice.

Kaa's Aloo Gobi

The always-ravenous Kaa isn't known for eating many vegetables. However, this vegetarian dish of cauliflower, potato, and a warm blend of spices just might entice him.

Directions

1. Ask an adult for help at the stove. In a large skillet over medium heat, warm the oil. Add the garlic, ginger, garam masala, cumin, turmeric, salt, and pepper. Cook 1 minute. Add the onion and cook until softened, about 3 minutes. Add the cauliflower and potatoes and continue to cook, stirring frequently, until beginning to soften, about 8 minutes. Add the tomatoes, using your hands to break them into small pieces, then stir to combine.

2. Add ⅓ cup water to the pan, cover, and continue to cook until the vegetables are softened, about 10 minutes more. Sprinkle with cilantro before serving.

Gaston's Chicken Drumsticks

These drumsticks would fit right in on the menu at Gaston's favorite tavern! They're the perfect dinner to satisfy a hearty appetite.

Directions

1. Ask an adult for help with the oven. Heat the oven to 425°F. Fit a baking sheet with a baking rack.

2. In a large bowl, toss together all the ingredients until the chicken is evenly coated. Arrange the pieces on the rack. Bake until golden and crispy, about 40 minutes. Serve immediately with lemon wedges.

Makes 8

Ingredients

8 chicken drumsticks

3 Tbsp olive oil

2 garlic cloves, grated

1 tsp lemon zest, plus lemon wedges for serving

2 Tbsp herbes de Provence

1½ tsp kosher salt

1 tsp black pepper

Tip

If you like them extra crispy, you can broil the drumsticks for 2 or 3 minutes after baking. Be sure to watch them carefully so they don't burn.

Serves 4

Ingredients

1 lb firm tofu, drained

⅓ cup flour

1½ tsp salt

¾ tsp garlic powder

¾ tsp onion powder

½ tsp paprika

2 Tbsp coconut aminos

1 Tbsp lemon juice

3 Tbsp soy milk

¾ cup panko bread crumbs

1 Tbsp vegetable oil

8 (snack-size) sheets nori, crumbled

Tip

Turn to page 132 *to learn how to cut your tofu sticks evenly without a ruler.*

Fishy Sticks

This recipe may resemble crunchy fish sticks, but it's actually made using tofu. Share these with unsuspecting friends or family and see how they react—a clever ruse not unlike Ursula's disguise as Vanessa, but with a much happier result!

Directions

1. Ask an adult for help with the oven. Heat the oven to 375°F. Line a baking sheet with parchment paper. Slice the tofu into 12 even pieces.

2. In a shallow bowl, combine the flour, 1 teaspoon salt, garlic powder, onion powder, and paprika. In another bowl, stir together the coconut aminos, lemon juice, and soy milk. In a third bowl, combine the panko and vegetable oil, then stir in the nori and remaining ½ teaspoon salt.

3. Dredge a tofu piece in the flour. Dip in the soy mixture, then gently toss in the panko mixture to evenly coat. Place on the baking sheet. Repeat with the remaining tofu pieces.

4. Bake the tofu 15 minutes, then flip and bake until golden and crunchy, about 15 minutes more. Let cool slightly before serving.

Dr. Facilier's Sheet Pan Shrimp Boil

Serves 4

Ingredients

2 tsp Old Bay seasoning

½ to 1 tsp Creole seasoning

¾ lb baby red potatoes

3 Tbsp olive oil

2 large ears corn, quartered

12 oz smoked andouille

½ lb large shrimp, peeled and deveined

This New Orleans–inspired seafood boil doesn't use any water! Instead of placing the spicy sausage, shrimp, and veggies in an oversized pot on the stove, they're spread onto a sheet pan and baked in the oven with the same flavorful, savory result.

Directions

1. Ask an adult for help with the oven. Heat the oven to 425°F. In a small bowl, stir together the Old Bay and Creole seasoning.

2. Toss the potatoes with one-third of the seasoning mix and 1 tablespoon oil. Spread the potatoes on a baking sheet and bake 20 minutes.

3. Toss the corn and andouille with one-third of the seasoning and 1 tablespoon oil. Add the mixture to the sheet pan and bake 10 minutes. Toss the shrimp and remaining seasoning mix with 1 tablespoon oil, then add to the same sheet pan and bake until the shrimp is pink and opaque, about 5 minutes. Serve immediately.

Tip

For a Facilier-themed feast, pair this recipe with the Blueberry Sparkler beverage **on page 94**.

Serves 6

Ingredients

Breadsticks

¾ to 1 lb
pizza dough

Flour, for dusting

1 Tbsp peppercorns

Stew

2 Tbsp olive oil

1 (14-oz)
package chorizo,
thinly sliced

1 large onion, chopped

3 garlic cloves,
minced

1½ tsp salt

¼ tsp pepper

4 cups chicken broth

3 medium Yukon
Gold potatoes,
peeled and cut into
1-inch cubes

½ large bunch
green kale, torn into
bite-size pieces
(about 6 cups)

1 (14-oz) can
white beans,
rinsed and drained

Serpent Stew

Just like Jafar and his serpent staff, these serpent-shaped breadsticks and stew make a powerful pair.

Directions

1. Ask an adult for help with the oven. Heat the oven to 400°F and line two baking sheets with parchment paper. Divide the dough into 8 to 10 portions. On a lightly floured surface, roll a portion into a 2-foot-long rope. Working directly on one of the prepared sheets, wind and shape the rope into a snake. Repeat with the remaining dough, spacing each snake 2 inches apart.

2. Press a pair of peppercorn eyes into each snake. Bake the snakes until golden and puffed, about 10 minutes. Set aside to cool.

3. Ask an adult for help at the stove. In a large pot over medium heat, warm the oil. Add the chorizo and cook until browned, about 8 minutes. Transfer the meat to a bowl. Add the onion to the pan and cook until softened, about 3 minutes. Add the garlic and cook 1 minute. Season with the salt and pepper, then add the broth and 3 cups water, and bring to a boil.

4. Place the potatoes in the pot and reduce the heat to a simmer. Continue to simmer until the potatoes are cooked through, about 12 minutes. Ask an adult for help with the blender. Remove half the stew from the pot and puree it in the blender. Add it back to the pot along with the kale and white beans, and return to a simmer. Cook until the kale is wilted, about 8 minutes. Serve each portion hot in a bowl topped with a snake breadstick.

Sides

Yzma's Roasted Broccoli with Parmesan

When one of Yzma's nefarious plans is foiled, she attempts to signal her sidekick, Kronk, for help using two stalks of broccoli. The florets in this recipe are sprinkled with fresh-squeezed lemon juice and Parmesan cheese—a combination far too tasty to waste on any shenanigans!

Directions

1. Ask an adult for help with the oven. Heat the oven to 450°F. On a large baking sheet, toss together the broccoli, olive oil, and salt. Roast the broccoli on the bottom rack until crisp, tender, and charred in spots, about 12 to 15 minutes, flipping halfway through.

2. With an adult's help, transfer the broccoli to a medium bowl and toss with the Parmesan and lemon juice. Serve immediately.

Serves 5

Ingredients

2 medium broccoli crowns (about 1½ lb), cut into florets

4 tsp olive oil

¼ tsp kosher salt

2 Tbsp grated Parmesan

1 Tbsp lemon juice

Tip

If you like, you can use crumbled feta cheese in this recipe in place of Parmesan.

Ingredients

1½ lb purple potatoes
(or a combination of red
and purple potatoes)

2 stalks celery, sliced

2 scallions, sliced

¼ cup mayonnaise

1 tsp Dijon mustard

1 Tbsp apple cider
vinegar

¼ tsp kosher salt

¼ tsp black pepper

2 Tbsp olive oil

1 Tbsp chopped
fresh dill

Tip

*Dill is the perfect
complement to this tasty
salad, but you
can also use parsley
or tarragon in its place.*

Maleficent's Purple Potato Salad

**Whether Maleficent is in human or dragon form, her
purple color scheme is hard to miss. This purple salad has
a traditional creamy lemon-and-herb-flavored dressing,
but it's dressed lightly to show off its unique hue.**

Directions

1. Ask an adult for help at the stove. Bring a large pot of salted
   water to a boil. Add the potatoes and cook until tender, about
   12 minutes. Drain, then transfer to a large bowl and cool
   completely. Once cooled, add the celery and scallions.

2. In a small bowl, combine the mayonnaise, mustard, vinegar,
   salt, pepper, olive oil, and dill. Whisk until well blended, then
   pour over the potato mixture. Stir to coat the vegetables evenly.
   Refrigerate until ready to serve.

Black and White Bean Salad

Can you guess which villain is most likely to enjoy this picnic-worthy side complete with two kinds of beans, sweet bell peppers, and a bright and citrusy homemade dressing? Here's a hint: the main ingredients match the colors of her extraordinary hair.

Directions

1. In a large bowl, combine the beans, bell pepper, shallot, and cilantro.

2. In a small bowl, whisk together the olive oil, paprika, lime juice, salt, and pepper.

3. Pour the dressing over the salad and toss to coat the vegetables evenly. Refrigerate until ready to serve.

Serves 6

Ingredients

1 (15-oz) can black beans, drained and rinsed

1 (15-oz) can cannellini beans, drained and rinsed

½ large red bell pepper, chopped

3 Tbsp chopped shallot

2 Tbsp chopped cilantro

5 Tbsp olive oil

¾ tsp smoked paprika

3 Tbsp lime juice

¾ tsp kosher salt

¼ tsp black pepper

Tip

This salad comes together quickly, but you can also make it a day ahead if you'd like.

Serves 6

Ingredients

½ of 1 cantaloupe

1 small dragon fruit

½ cup blueberries

½ cup raspberries

½ cup green grapes

Juice of ½ lime

1 Tbsp honey

1 small star fruit, sliced
(optional)

Tip

*If you can't find
star fruit, you can
substitute your own
favorite fruit by
cutting it into thick slices,
then using a star-shaped
food cutter to shape it.*

Ursula's Sea Bubble Berry Salad

A melon baller—a small round spoon made for scooping—gives some of the fruit in this rainbow salad a round shape, just like the bubbles swirling around Ursula's ocean lair.

Directions

1. Use a melon baller to scoop the cantaloupe and place the fruit in a large bowl. With an adult's help, halve the dragon fruit. Use the melon baller once more to shape the fruit, and add it to the bowl with the cantaloupe. Gently toss in the blueberries, raspberries, and grapes.

2. In a small bowl, stir together the lime juice and honey. Pour the mixture over the fruit and stir until combined. Refrigerate until ready to serve. Right before serving, garnish the salad with star fruit.

Jafar's Jewel Salad

Sparkling gems aren't just a part of Jafar's regal attire—he also uses them as tools to achieve his ultimate goal of becoming sultan. This bright salad features jewel-toned vegetables, making it an enticing and colorful dish.

Ingredients

1½ cups cooked bulgur, cooled

½ small yellow bell pepper, chopped

3 Tbsp chopped red onion

2 Persian cucumbers, chopped

1 cup cherry tomatoes, halved

2 Tbsp chopped parsley

2 Tbsp lemon juice

¼ cup olive oil

¾ tsp kosher salt

¼ tsp black pepper

Directions

1. In a large bowl, combine the bulgur, bell pepper, red onion, cucumbers, tomatoes, and parsley.

2. In another small bowl, whisk together the lemon juice, olive oil, salt, and pepper. Pour the dressing over the salad and toss to coat. Refrigerate until ready to serve.

Tip

Bulgur has a slightly nutty flavor and pleasantly chewy texture similar to brown rice. It is found in lots of dishes traditionally prepared in the Middle East.

Snacks

Ingredients

2 tsp olive oil

1 small leek, white and pale-green parts only, finely chopped

½ cup grape tomatoes, chopped

2 tsp chopped fresh basil

¼ tsp kosher salt

¼ tsp black pepper

1 refrigerated piecrust from a 15-oz package

2 oz goat cheese

1 egg

Tip

A pastry tamper can make the job of shaping dough for tarts much easier. (If you don't own a pastry tamper, you can use a teaspoon or even your fingers to mold/tamp down the pastry.)

Queen of Hearts Tomato Tarts

Wonderland is known for its extravagant tea parties—and its size-changing foods! The Queen of Hearts would surely love this small tart that features a heart shape and her favorite color, red.

Directions

1. Ask an adult for help with the oven. Heat the oven to 400°F. In a small skillet over medium heat, warm the olive oil. Add the leek and cook until tender, about 5 minutes. Place in a small bowl and combine with the tomatoes, basil, salt, and pepper. Set aside.

2. Use a 2½-inch round cookie cutter to shape 18 circles from the piecrust dough, then shape 18 hearts from the remaining scraps with a mini heart cutter. When needed, gather and reroll the dough to ¼-inch thickness as you work.

3. Use a pastry tamper to mold each dough round in a well of a mini cupcake pan. Evenly divide the goat cheese among the tarts, followed by the tomato mixture. Top each tart with a dough heart.

4. In a small bowl, whisk the egg with 1 tablespoon water. Brush the tarts with the egg wash, then bake until light golden brown, about 12 minutes. Serve warm.

Towering Parfait

If there's one place Mother Gothel knows best, it's the tall tower she lives in! This tasty snack, featuring towering layers of pudding, fruit, and whipped cream, is a delicious take on her memorable home.

Directions

1. Spoon a little pudding into the bottoms of two parfait glasses. Top the pudding with a layer of fresh berries, followed by a big dollop of whipped cream.

2. Repeat step 1.

3. Add one more layer of pudding.

4. Top each parfait with a small dollop of whipped cream and garnish, if you like, with 1 or 2 fresh berries.

Makes 2

Ingredients

Lemon or vanilla low-fat pudding

Fresh blueberries or blackberries

Whipped cream

Tip

For another yummy version of this snack, make it with lemon yogurt in place of the pudding.

Ingredients

6 large eggs

2 Tbsp mayonnaise

½ ripe avocado, diced

Kosher salt

Black pepper

3 mini kosher dill
pickles

Tip

*Steaming the eggs
rather than boiling
them makes peeling
the shells a snap!
If you need more guidance
on how to peel eggs,*
check out page 133.

Croco-Deviled Eggs

Captain Hook would never willingly approach a crocodile—
but he just might enjoy these most *egg*-cellent stuffed eggs.
Avocado gives them their green hue, while tiny slices of pickle
provide their reptilian appearance.

Directions

1. Fill a large pot with 1 inch of water and fit a steaming basket
   inside. Ask an adult for help at the stove. Bring the water to a
   boil over medium-high heat.

2. Ask an adult to carefully place the eggs in the steaming basket.
   Steam 14 minutes. Just before the eggs are done, prepare an
   ice bath. Ask an adult to transfer the eggs to the ice bath.
   Cool 10 minutes.

3. Tap and gently roll each egg on your work surface to make
   cracks. Peel off the shells, then, with an adult's help, halve the
   eggs lengthwise.

4. Drop the yolk from each egg half into a small bowl. Arrange
   the empty egg whites on a plate. Add the mayonnaise, avocado,
   and ¼ tsp each salt and pepper to the bowl with the yolks, and
   use a fork to mash and blend the mixture until smooth. Taste
   and adjust seasoning if you like, adding more mayonnaise for
   a creamier texture or salt and pepper for more flavor. Add a
   spoonful of filling to each egg white.

5. Trim the pickles into claws, as shown, and press them in place
   on the eggs.

Octo-Arm Breadsticks

Fashioned after Ursula's tentacle-like arms, these snaky breadsticks are embellished with black olive suction cups and sprinkled with cheese.

Directions

1. First make the sauce. Ask an adult for help at the stove. Warm the oil in a small skillet over medium heat. Add the shallot and cook until softened, about 2 minutes. Stir in the garlic, oregano, salt, and pepper and cook 1 minute. Add the tomatoes, breaking them into small pieces with your hands. Reduce the heat to low and simmer 10 minutes to let the flavors meld. Ask an adult for help with the immersion blender. Transfer the mixture to a bowl, then use the blender to partially puree into a chunky sauce. Cover and set aside.

2. Ask an adult for help with the oven. Heat the oven to 400°F. Line two baking sheets with parchment paper. Unroll the dough on a lightly floured cutting board. Use a pizza cutter to evenly slice the dough into 8 strips. Roll each strip into a long, ½-inch-thick rope. Place 4 ropes on each sheet, spacing them 2 inches apart. Shape them into coily tentacles, as shown.

3. In a small bowl, whisk the egg with 1 tablespoon water. Brush each breadstick with the egg wash, then flatten each one slightly and press olive slices into each, as shown. Bake until light golden, about 10 minutes. Brush the breadsticks with butter and sprinkle with Parmesan. Serve immediately with the marinara on the side for dipping.

Makes 8 breadsticks and a generous cup of marinara

Ingredients

Marinara Sauce
1 Tbsp olive oil

1 large shallot, roughly chopped

1 garlic clove, pressed

1 tsp dried oregano

½ tsp kosher salt

¼ tsp black pepper

6 whole canned tomatoes

Breadsticks
Flour, for dusting

1 (8-oz) package refrigerated thin-crust pizza dough

1 egg

Sliced black olives

2 Tbsp butter, melted

2 Tbsp grated Parmesan

Tip

These breadsticks are best served warm, right out of the oven.

Ingredients

16 whole pitted dates

¼ cup golden raisins

¼ cup toasted unsalted
sunflower seeds

½ cup roasted and
salted cashews

2 Tbsp unsweetened
finely shredded coconut

¼ cup dark
chocolate chips

1 tsp vegetable oil

Tip

*If preferred, you can
use semisweet chips
in place of the
dark chocolate
for drizzling.*

Striped Tiger Bites

All the animals in the jungle recognize the fearsome Shere Khan's distinctive stripes. Satisfy a growling belly with these fruit, nut, and seed squares "striped" with drizzles of chocolate.

Directions

1. Line a loaf pan with parchment paper, using enough to cover the edges of the pan. With an adult's help, combine the dates, raisins, sunflower seeds, cashews, and coconut in the bowl of a food processor. Pulse the mixture until it holds together but still has some small, uniform bits.

2. Spoon the mixture into the prepared loaf pan. Use another small sheet of parchment to press the mixture so that it forms an even layer. Refrigerate 1 hour.

3. Grab the edges of the parchment paper to lift the bar from the pan and place it on a cutting board. Working on the parchment and with an adult's help, use a sharp knife to cut the bar crosswise into 6 even strips. Slice each strip into 3 even squares.

4. In a microwave-safe bowl, combine the chocolate chips and vegetable oil. Microwave on half power for 1 minute, then stir (be careful, the bowl and its contents will be very hot) to encourage melting. If needed, return the chocolate to the microwave and heat in 10-second bursts until melted, stirring vigorously between each heating. Let the chocolate cool slightly, then place in a resealable bag and snip a corner.

5. Drizzle the melted chocolate onto the squares by gently squeezing it from the bag. Let the chocolate set before serving or packaging. Keep refrigerated until ready to eat.

Iago's Crunchy Seed Clusters

Iago has had his fill of crackers, but we bet he'd peck at these oven-toasted clusters with almonds, pepitas, and a mix of flavorful seeds. Maple syrup, vanilla, and shredded coconut add a touch of sweetness.

Directions

1. Ask an adult for help with the oven. Heat the oven to 325°F and line a baking sheet with parchment paper. In a small bowl, stir together the maple syrup, vanilla, egg white, and salt. Set aside. In a large bowl, combine all the remaining ingredients. Stir to evenly coat the mixture with the oil. Add the egg mixture and stir to coat.

2. Spread the mixture on the prepared baking sheet in an even layer. Bake 20 minutes, then have an adult use a spatula to flip the mixture (it's okay if it breaks into smaller pieces). Bake 8 minutes more. Let cool completely on the pan (it will crisp up as it cools) before breaking into bite-size pieces.

Serves 8

Ingredients

¼ cup maple syrup

1¼ tsp vanilla extract

1 egg white

¾ tsp kosher salt

½ cup raw sunflower seeds

2 Tbsp sesame seeds

2 Tbsp flax seeds

⅓ cup raw pepitas

1 cup raw almonds

¼ cup pine nuts

⅔ cup unsweetened shredded coconut

2 Tbsp unrefined coconut oil, melted

Tip

For the best results, be sure not to overbake the clusters or they may turn bitter. The ingredients should look toasty but not dark brown.

Beverages

Serves 4

Ingredients

4 cups of your favorite prepared lemonade (a light-colored drink works best), chilled

Blue food coloring

Lemon slices, for garnish

Special Equipment

Star-shaped ice or food mold

Night Howler Lemonade

Deputy Mayor Dawn Bellwether uses the strange Night Howler flower to make trouble in Zootopia! Inspired by the flower's bright color, this blue lemonade is a more dramatic take on a classic summer drink.

Directions

1. Fill the mold with water and freeze until solid, about 3 hours.

2. In a large pitcher, stir together the lemonade with 2 drops food coloring. If needed, add another drop or two to reach the desired hue.

3. Evenly divide the drink into glasses and add a few star ice cubes. Garnish with lemon slices and serve.

Blueberry Sparkler

Just like Dr. Facilier, you can easily make your own homemade potion—a bubbly violet-colored soda that is refreshing and fun to drink.

Directions

1. Use a vegetable peeler to remove half the rind from the lemon. Ask an adult for help at the stove. Place the rind in a large saucepan, along with the blueberries, ginger, sugar, and 2 cups of water (regular, not sparkling). Bring to a boil, then reduce the heat to low and simmer 20 minutes. Let cool completely.

2. Strain the syrup into a clean jar. To make each sparkler, fill an 8-ounce glass with ice. Add 2 tablespoons syrup, then top off with seltzer or sparkling water. If you'd like, garnish with fresh blueberries and a lemon slice. Serve immediately.

Serves about 16

Ingredients

1 lemon

3 cups blueberries, plus more for garnish

1 (1-inch) piece fresh ginger, sliced

1½ cups sugar

Ice

Plain seltzer or sparkling water

Lemon slices for garnish (optional)

Tip

The outermost part of a citrus rind (also called zest) can be used to add lots of flavor to a recipe. Here it's used to make the syrup taste lemony. Don't know how to remove zest? **Check out the Glossary on page 141 for instructions.**

Ingredients

Green liquid food coloring (optional)

12 oz green or clear lemon-lime soda

4 scoops lemon or lime sorbet

Sour candies or gumdrops for garnish

2 bamboo skewers

Tip

A slice of fruit would make a fun garnish for this float, too.

Sour Bill's Citrus Float

Scoops of fruit sorbet and fizzy lemon-lime soda make this foamy concoction both sweet and sour—just like Sour Bill. To feel like you're inside the game of *Sugar Rush*, you can garnish each glass with gumdrops and sour candies.

Directions

1. In a tall glass, stir together a drop of food coloring, if using, with a splash of soda. Add 2 scoops sorbet, then top off with half the remaining soda. Repeat with a second glass.

2. Ask an adult for help with threading a few candies onto each skewer (be careful of the sharp point). Slide a skewer into each glass. Enjoy immediately.

Savanna Sunset Slushie

Makes 2

Even Scar's dark plot to become king can't cast a shadow over the glowing Pride Lands sunset. This icy pink-and-gold slushie captures its colorful beauty and makes a refreshing treat on a warm summer day.

Directions

1. Ask an adult for help with the blender. In the blender, combine the orange juice concentrate with 2 cups of ice and 6 tablespoons water. Blend into a slush, then divide evenly between two glasses.

2. Rinse the blender's pitcher with cool water, then add the pink lemonade concentrate, remaining 2 cups ice, and 6 tablespoons water. Puree into slush. Add half the mixture to each glass. Use a straw to gently blend the edges of the slushie layers in each glass, as shown. Top each with a cherry. Serve immediately.

Ingredients

¼ cup frozen orange juice concentrate

4 cups ice

¼ cup frozen pink lemonade concentrate

2 maraschino cherries with stems, for garnish

Tip

Make this drink extra special by serving it in a fancy glass. Just be sure it has see-through sides!

Ingredients

4 cups apple cider

2 cinnamon sticks, plus more for garnish

6 orange slices, plus more for garnish

4 star anise pods

4 whole cloves

1 Tbsp honey (optional)

Tip

Serve the cider with your favorite pastry.

Witch's Brew

The Queen is known for brewing a mixture that casts a sleepy spell. But a mug of this steamy drink—made with apple cider, oranges, and spices—is simply warm and cozy! Letting the mixture steep for several minutes after the cider simmers will add more flavor.

Directions

1. Ask an adult for help at the stove. In a medium saucepan, combine the cider, cinnamon sticks, orange slices, star anise, and cloves. Warm over medium heat until the mixture begins to bubble around the edges. Reduce the heat to low and simmer 20 minutes. Turn off the heat and let sit 5 minutes more. Stir in the honey, if using.

2. Set a mesh strainer over a bowl. With an adult's help, pour the cider through the strainer and discard the solids. Pour the cider into mugs and garnish each with a cinnamon stick and orange slice. Serve warm.

Chocolate Mud Puddle

Serves 2

The last thing Gaston wants to do is soil his beautiful appearance! But sometimes his actions land him in muddy waters. This cup of hot cocoa topped with mini marshmallows offers an edible homage with its own surprise twist: chocolate hazelnut spread.

Ingredients

1 Tbsp cocoa powder, plus more for garnish

2 cups milk of your choice

3 Tbsp chocolate hazelnut spread

Marshmallows, for garnish

Directions

1. In a medium saucepan, whisk together the cocoa powder and ½ cup milk until the cocoa is dissolved. Ask an adult for help at the stove. Stir in the remaining 1½ cups milk and the hazelnut spread, then set over medium heat. Warm until the mixture is hot and the hazelnut spread has dissolved, about 3 minutes.

2. With an adult's help, pour the cocoa into mugs. Garnish each with marshmallows and a sprinkle of cocoa powder. Serve immediately.

Tip

Pack this cocoa in a thermos and bring it along on a hike for a warming treat. It can easily be doubled so there's plenty to share.

Sweets

Chocolate Top Hats

Ingredients

8 chocolate wafer
cookies

6 oz dark or semisweet
chocolate, chopped

2 tsp vegetable oil

8 large marshmallows

2 strips red sour tape
candy

8 purple neon banana
candies

¼ cup white frosting

Special Equipment
Toothpicks

Tip

*To help the chocolate
set quicker,
place the hats in
the refrigerator
for 10 minutes
at the end of step 3.*

Dr. Facilier is rarely seen without his signature top hat!
This treat, styled as the villain's infamous chapeau, conceals
a sweet secret—a puffy marshmallow under an irresistible
layer of chocolate.

Directions

1. Arrange the cookies on a baking sheet in a single layer. Fill a
   saucepan with 1 inch of water and set a heat-safe bowl over the
   top, making sure the bottom of the bowl does not touch the
   water. Add the chocolate to the bowl.

2. Ask an adult for help at the stove. Heat the saucepan with the
   bowl on medium heat. Melt the chocolate, stirring frequently so
   that it heats evenly. Once melted, remove from the heat and stir
   in the vegetable oil.

3. Stand a marshmallow on the end of a fork. Working over the
   bowl with the melted chocolate, spoon the chocolate over the
   marshmallow to cover the top and sides. Gently tap the fork
   on the side of the bowl to remove the
   excess chocolate, then use a toothpick
   to slide the marshmallow onto one
   of the cookies. Repeat with the
   remaining marshmallows, chocolate,
   and cookies. Let the chocolate set.

4. Trim the tape candy into
   8 strips. Use the frosting
   to attach a strip and
   purple banana "feather"
   to each hat, as shown.

Flame Meringue Pops

When Hades is in a good mood, the flames atop his head are a cool blue—but make him angry, and they'll quickly roar to orange and red! These pops were designed with Hades's calmer state in mind, but should the feeling strike, you can replace the blue with a fierier color.

Directions

1. Ask an adult for help with the oven. Heat the oven to 200°F and line two baking sheets with parchment paper. In a stand mixer fitted with a whisk attachment and set on medium speed, whip the egg whites with the cream of tartar, vanilla, and salt until frothy. Add a tablespoon sugar, increase the mixer's speed to medium high, and continue to whip until the sugar is dissolved. Keep adding the sugar 1 tablespoon at a time, letting the sugar dissolve between each addition, until stiff peaks form and all the sugar has been added, about 12 minutes.

2. Add a few drops of food coloring to the meringue and gently stir a few times to swirl, but do not fully blend the color. Transfer the mixture to a piping bag fitted with a large star tip.

3. Lay a lollipop stick 3 inches from the edge of one of the prepared pans. Hold the stick in place and pipe the meringue in a flame pattern, as shown, covering the top 2 inches of the stick. Repeat with the remaining sticks and meringue.

4. Bake the pops for 2 hours, then turn off the heat and let them cool completely in the oven, about 2 hours more. To prevent cracking, do not open the oven door as they cook or cool.

Makes 6 to 8

Ingredients

2 egg whites

⅛ tsp cream of tartar

¼ tsp vanilla extract

Pinch kosher salt

½ cup sugar

Blue food coloring
(or other color of choice)

6-inch lollipop sticks

Tip

Check out page 134 for a visual guide to creating these pops—and page 140 for more information about piping bags!

Ingredients

1¼ cups white frosting

Red food coloring

4 chocolate chew candies

12 plain cupcakes

12 large white gumdrops

12 small white gumdrops

24 white Jordan almonds

24 white pearl sprinkles

12 jumbo star sprinkles

Tip

Experiment with different colors, shapes, and sizes of candy to create a castle of your own design.

Sugar Rush Castle Cupcakes

King Candy's home-sweet-home comes to life with this fanciful cupcake. Pearl sprinkles and sugar-coated gumdrops give this edible castle some extra sparkle.

Directions

1. Tint 1 cup of the frosting pink with the red food coloring. Use your fingers to flatten each chocolate chew candy and trim 3 small doors from each, as shown.

2. Working with one cupcake at a time, cover the top with pink frosting. Press on a large white gumdrop, then use some of the remaining white frosting to attach a small white gumdrop on top. Stand a Jordan almond on each side of the white gumdrop, as shown, then top each almond with a white pearl sprinkle. Finish the castle with a chocolate door and star sprinkle top (attached with frosting). Repeat with the remaining cupcakes and ingredients.

Black Cat Doughnuts

Lady Tremaine's loyal pet, Lucifer, is purr-fectly captured in this plain doughnut turned decorated dessert, right down to his mischievous grin. It's best served with a glass of milk, of course!

Directions

1. Use the food writers to draw an eye and pupil in the center of each Jordan almond, as shown. Place 3 tablespoons of the chocolate frosting and all the white frosting in separate piping bags, each fitted with a small writing tip. Place the remaining chocolate frosting in a piping bag fitted with a mini star tip.

2. Using the chocolate frosting in the bag with the star tip, cover the top half of each doughnut with tiny dots of frosting, as shown. Press a pair of almond eyes and a pink jelly bean nose onto each. Trim the rounded chocolate end from each almond, and attach them with chocolate frosting, as shown. Use the white frosting to pipe a center in each ear.

3. Using the chocolate frosting in the bag with the writing tip, draw a mouth on each doughnut, as shown. Finish by piping on white frosting whiskers.

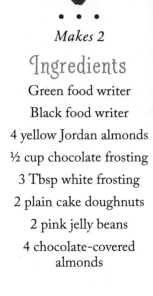

Makes 2

Ingredients

Green food writer

Black food writer

4 yellow Jordan almonds

½ cup chocolate frosting

3 Tbsp white frosting

2 plain cake doughnuts

2 pink jelly beans

4 chocolate-covered almonds

Tip

A food writer is a marker that is filled with edible ink. You can find them online or at craft or cooking stores that sell baking supplies.

Makes 18

Ingredients

3 Tbsp granulated
sugar, plus more
for rolling

½ tsp ground cinnamon

1 sheet puff pastry
dough (from a 17-oz
package)

3 Tbsp butter, melted

1 Tbsp coarse sugar

Special Equipment
Toothpicks

Tip

Turn to page 135
*for step-by-step
instructions on how
to shape these
special treats.*

Elephant Ears

The hyenas Shenzi, Banzai, and Ed serve as loyal minions to the nefarious Scar, aiding in his plot to rule over the animal kingdom. The trio can often be found in the Elephant Graveyard on the edges of the Pride Lands—but this delicious dessert is a lighter homage to their shadowy stomping grounds.

Directions

1. Ask an adult for help with the oven. Heat the oven to 400°F and line two baking sheets with parchment paper. In a small bowl, stir together the sugar and cinnamon.

2. Sprinkle your work surface with sugar. Using a rolling pin or similar tool, roll the dough out into a 12-inch square. Brush it generously with butter and sprinkle with the cinnamon sugar. Roll once more to press the sugar into the dough. Use a toothpick to make a small mark in the center of the square. Starting at one end, roll the dough up into a tube, stopping at the center mark. Repeat with the opposite side of the dough to form a tube with two curled sides.

3. With an adult's help, cut the tube crosswise into ½-inch-thick slices. Arrange on the baking sheets, spreading them 2 inches apart. Brush them with the remaining butter and sprinkle with coarse sugar. Bake until crisp and puffed, about 10 minutes. Let cool before serving.

Treasure Trove Coconut Ice Cream

This rich and creamy no-churn ice cream is filled with delicious treasures, including chocolate chunks and toasted coconut. Be sure to use cream of coconut, a sugary flavored syrup used in drinks and desserts, rather than coconut cream for flavoring.

Directions

1. Ask an adult for help with the oven. Heat the oven to 350°F. Spread the shredded coconut on a baking sheet. Toast it until light golden, about 8 to 10 minutes. Transfer it immediately to a plate and let it cool completely.

2. In a large bowl, whisk together the sweetened condensed milk and cream of coconut. In another bowl, use a hand mixer set on medium speed to whip the heavy cream until stiff peaks form, about 2 minutes. Gently fold the whipped cream into the milk mixture, being careful not to deflate it by mixing too long.

3. Set aside 2 tablespoons of the chocolate chunks. Fold the remaining chocolate into the cream, then fold in the coconut. Pour the mixture into a loaf pan. Gently smooth the top with the back of a spoon, then sprinkle with the reserved chocolate.

4. Cover the ice cream with plastic wrap, then freeze until solid, about 6 hours.

Serves 8

Ingredients

½ cup shredded sweetened coconut

1 (14-oz) can sweetened condensed milk

3 Tbsp cream of coconut

1¾ cups heavy cream

½ cup chocolate chunks, roughly chopped

Tip

No ice cream machine?
No problem!
The only equipment you'll need to make this dessert is a hand mixer.

117

Ingredients

1 (16-oz) package
refrigerated sugar
cookie dough

6 Tbsp flour

2 cups powdered sugar,
sifted

4 tsp meringue powder

1 Tbsp light
corn syrup

Edible silver dust

Gold sprinkles

Tip

*If you've made other
desserts in this book,
you may already be
familiar with a
piping bag!
But if not,* **check out
page 140** *for more info.*

Magic Mirror Sugar Cookies

You won't see your reflection in these cookies, but their silver and gold embellishments are nearly as enchanting as the Magic Mirror that speaks to the Queen. You'll need some time and patience to make a batch, but the end result will be nothing short of bewitching.

Directions

1. Ask an adult for help with the oven. Heat the oven to 350°F and line two baking sheets with parchment paper. In a large bowl, break the dough into several pieces, then toss with the flour. Use your hands to knead the flour into the dough.

2. On a lightly floured surface, roll the dough out to ¼-inch thickness. Use a 2 ½-to 3-inch oval cookie cutter to shape the dough. Arrange the cookies on a prepared baking sheet, spacing them 2 inches apart. Gather and reroll the dough as needed. Freeze the unbaked cookies 10 minutes.

3. Bake the cookies until light golden on the bottom, about 12 minutes. Let cool on the pan for 5 minutes, then transfer to a rack to cool completely.

4. Once the cookies have cooled, use a hand mixer to blend together the powdered sugar, meringue powder, and corn syrup with ¼ cup water until thickened. If the icing is too stiff, add 1 more teaspoon of water and stir once again (up to 3 teaspoons can be added, if needed). Transfer the mixture to a piping bag fitted with a writing tip.

5. Use the icing to pipe an oval in the center of each cookie, leaving a ½-inch border. Let dry, then brush with silver dust. Use the remaining icing to attach gold sprinkles around the edge of each cookie. Let the icing set several hours before serving.

Captain Hook Brownie Bites

Reel in your crew with a chocolaty delight that recalls one of Hook's most memorable features.

Directions

1. Line a baking sheet with parchment paper. Combine the candy melts in a small microwave-safe bowl, and melt according to the package directions. Transfer the candy to a piping bag fitted with a small writing tip, then pipe 12 hook shapes onto the prepared pan. Let the candy set.

2. Meanwhile, place ½ cup frosting in a small bowl and add in the red food coloring. Transfer it to a piping bag fitted with a large round tip. Place the remaining frosting in a piping bag fitted with a large star tip.

3. Pipe a large dollop of red frosting onto the top of each brownie bite by centering the piping tip atop the brownie, holding it ¼ inch from the surface, and pushing the frosting out so that it spreads to form a circle, as shown. Repeat the technique to add a dollop of white frosting to each brownie. Finish by adding a candy hook to each. Keep cool until ready to serve.

Makes 12

Ingredients

⅓ cup white candy melts

6 black candy melts

1½ cups white frosting

Red gel food coloring

12 store-bought brownie bites

Tip

If you like, you can replace the brownie bites in this recipe with mini chocolate cupcakes.

Ingredients

⅓ cup dark
chocolate chips

⅓ cup green candy
melts

24 plain chocolate
wafer cookies

12 jumbo heart sprinkles

½ cup your favorite
chocolate frosting

Tip

*To let something "set"
means to let it harden!
Be patient when the
chocolate is cooling to
ensure you're getting
the special shapes for
this cookie just right.*

Maleficent's Triple Chocolate Sandwich Cookies

Mesmerize chocolate lovers with a spellbinding sweet that looks just like Maleficent! These cookies come together like magic and feature chocolate both inside and out.

Directions

1. Line a baking sheet with parchment paper. Melt the chocolate chips according to the package directions and transfer to a piping bag fitted with a small writing tip. Pipe 12 sets of horns, as shown, onto the parchment. Let the chocolate set.

2. Meanwhile, in a small, heat-safe bowl, melt the green candy melts according to the package directions. Place the melted candy in a piping bag fitted with a small writing tip and use it to create the outline of Maleficent's face on 12 of the cookies. Let set 3 minutes. Working with one cookie at a time, use the melted candy to fill in the center of the face and quickly place a heart sprinkle near the bottom, as shown. Repeat with the remaining candy and sprinkles. Let set completely.

3. Spread 2 teaspoons frosting onto each of the remaining cookies. Press a set of chocolate horns into the frosting at the top edge of the cookie, then sandwich with a cookie face.

Cruella Cookies

The sleek black-and-white coloring on these sugar cookies comes from dipping them in chocolate—a decadent tribute to the very fashionable Cruella.

Directions

1. Ask an adult for help with the oven. Heat the oven to 350°F and line two baking sheets with parchment paper. Roll out the cookie dough to ¼-inch thickness. Use a 2½- to 3-inch round cutter to shape the dough into circles. Arrange them on the baking sheets, spacing them 2 inches apart. Gather and reroll the dough as needed.

2. Bake the cookies until set and slightly crisp, about 12 minutes, turning them once halfway through. Let the cookies cool on the pans for 5 minutes, then transfer them to a rack to cool completely. Cover the baking sheets with fresh paper and set aside.

3. Melt the white chocolate chips in a heat-safe bowl according to the package directions. Dip the edge of each cookie into the white chocolate, as shown, letting the excess fall back into the bowl. If needed, use the flat edge of a butter knife to scrape away any extra chocolate from the backs of the cookies. Place the cookies on a prepared baking sheet and let the chocolate set. Repeat the steps with the dark chocolate, dipping the opposite side. Attach a heart sprinkle mouth to each cookie with a bit of melted chocolate applied with a toothpick. Let set completely before serving.

Makes about 36

Ingredients

1 batch sugar cookie dough (store-bought or using your favorite recipe)

1 cup white chocolate chips

1 cup dark chocolate chips

Jumbo heart sprinkles

Ingredients

8 large strawberries

Whipped cream

Tip

Turn to page 136
*for step-by-step
instructions on how
to create the rose shape.
Don't worry if it's not
perfect—the result will
still be delicious!*

Edible Roses

The Queen of Hearts prefers that the roses in her garden are always red. Fortunately, these edible strawberry roses are red, too—with a dash of white whipped cream for delicious flavor.

Directions

1. Wash the strawberries in cold water and pat them dry with a paper towel.

2. Ask an adult to help you with the knife. Then slice off the strawberries' leafy tops.

3. Stand one of berries flat side (stem side) down. Create an outer row of 4 rose petals around the tip by slicing three-quarters of the way down through the berry on all 4 sides.

4. To finish the rose, cut a second strawberry in half from top to bottom. Then cut one of the halves into several slices. Tuck 3 or 4 of the slices between the tip and outer petals of the first berry.

5. Repeat with the remaining strawberries. Store any leftover strawberry pieces in the refrigerator to enjoy as a snack later.

6. Put a spoonful of whipped cream onto a plate. Set a strawberry rose on top, then repeat with remaining berries and whipped cream and serve.

Step-by-Step Instructions

Villains know that crafting the perfect potions and brews takes practice! Turn the page for step-by-step photos for some of the recipes—and you'll be a pro at creating dishes that are both delicious and eye-catching in no time.

Baguette Breakfast Beaks

Prep your baguette for a tasty baked-egg filling with this step-by-step guide.

1. Have an adult use a serrated knife to trim a rectangle from the center of the loaf, leaving a ½-inch border and being careful not to cut all the way through.

2. Pull away the rectangle of bread and discard or use to make croutons for another time.

See the full recipe on page 20!

Mini Tamatoa Seaweed Rolls

Roll up a satisfying veggie snack with this step-by-step guide.

1. Cover a sheet of nori with rice.

2. Add a few slices of each vegetable to the center of the roll.

3. Bring one end of the nori up and over the vegetables, as shown.

4. Continue to roll the nori until a cone is formed.

See the full recipe on page 34!

131

Fishy Sticks

Cut perfectly portioned sticks without a ruler using this step-by-step guide.

1. With an adult's help, stand the tofu on a short end and use a sharp knife to halve it lengthwise.

2. Lay the tofu down and, keeping the pieces stacked, halve it once more. You should now have 4 pieces total, 2 on top and 2 on bottom of stack.

3. Slice each stacked half into 3 pieces. You should now have 12 pieces total, six on top and six on bottom of stack.

4. The final 12 pieces should now look like the photo above.

See the full recipe on page 82!

Croco-Deviled Eggs

Crack and peel a hard-boiled egg with ease using this step-by-step guide.

1. Tap the large end of a hard-boiled egg on your work surface to crack it.

2. Lay the egg on its side and make several more cracks. Turn it a few times to make cracks all the way around the shell.

3. Use your fingers to roll the egg back and forth to make even more cracks.

4. Starting at the large end of the egg, peel away the shell, making sure to get underneath the membrane between the shell and egg. It should come off in large strips.

See the full recipe on page 82!

Flame Meringue Pops

Pipe the perfect pop with this step-by-step guide.

1. Use one hand to hold a lollipop stick in place. Use the other hand to pipe the meringue onto the stick, starting 2 inches from the top.

2. Continue to pipe the meringue, making sure each strip is connected. For more dimension layer a few dollops of meringue on top of the other strips.

See the full recipe on page 108!

Elephant Ears

Roll and slice a batch of irresistible cinnamon-sugar pastries with this step-by-step guide.

1. Roll the dough out into a 12-inch square and cover it in butter and cinnamon sugar.

2. Use a toothpick to mark the center of the square.

3. Starting at one end, roll the dough to the center of the square up to the hatch mark.

4. Repeat with the other side.

5. Cut the tube crosswise into ½-inch-thick slices.

Go to page 114 for the full recipe!

Edible Roses

Create edible blooms with this step-by-step guide.

1. With an adult's help, use a paring knife to trim the top from a strawberry.

2. Make 4 slits around the base of the berry, taking care not to cut all the way through. Set the berry aside.

3. Trim a second berry into very thin slices.

4. Layer the berry slices in the slits of the prepared berry to create petals.

Go to page 126 for the full recipe!

Dietary Considerations

Food allergies or preferences? No problem! Use this guide to check which recipes accommodate dairy-free, gluten-free, vegan, and vegetarian diets—and which can be adapted to let everyone enjoy the meal. Recipes not included below may not be suitable for special diets. If using store-bought ingredients, always check the label or packaging to make sure they meet your dietary needs.

DF = Dairy-Free (no milk products, but can include eggs) / GF = Gluten-Free / V = Vegan / VEG = Vegetarian

Breakfast

The Queen's Bewitching Apple Bowl   DF / GF / V / VEG
Spotted Scones   VEG
Rosy Red Oatmeal   DF / GF (if made with gluten-free oats) / V / VEG
Dozen-Egg Frittata   GF / VEG
Blackberry French Toast Casserole   VEG

Lunch

Kronk's Spinach Puffs   VEG
Smoky Chicken Salad Cups   DF / GF / V or VEG (if chicken and mayo are substituted with vegan alternatives)
Mini Tamatoa Seaweed Rolls   DF / GF / V / VEG
Roaring Pizza Pockets   VEG (if pepperoni is substituted with a vegetarian alternative)
Playing-Card Sandwiches   DF / GF (if made with gluten-free bread) / V / VEG
Golden Squash and Apple Soup   GF / V (if chicken broth and butter are substituted with vegan equivalents) / VEG (if made with vegetable broth)
Lady Tremaine's Emerald Grain Bowl   DF / GF / V (if honey is replaced with maple syrup) / VEG

Dinner

Captain Hook's Stuffed Shells   VEG
Spiced Chicken Kebabs   GF
Shape-Shifting Pesto Pasta   DF (if regular Parmesan is substituted with a vegan alternative) / GF (if made with gluten-free pasta) / VEG (if sausage is substituted with veggie alternative)
Kaa's Aloo Gobi   DF / GF / V / VEG
Gaston's Chicken Drumsticks   DF / GF
Fishy Sticks   DF / GF (if made with gluten-free panko and gluten-free flour) / V / VEG
Dr. Facilier's Sheet Pan Shrimp Boil   DF / GF
Serpent Stew   DF

Sides

Yzma's Roasted Broccoli with Parmesan   GF / V (if regular Parmesan is substituted with a vegan alternative) / VEG
Maleficent's Purple Potato Salad   DF / GF / V (if mayo is substituted with a vegan alternative) / VEG
Black and White Bean Salad   DF / GF / V / VEG
Ursula's Sea Bubble Berry Salad   DF / GF / V (if honey is replaced with maple syrup) / VEG
Jafar's Jewel Salad   DF / V / VEG

Snacks

Queen of Hearts Tomato Tarts   VEG
Towering Parfait   GF / VEG
Croco-Deviled Eggs   DF / GF / VEG
Octo-Arm Breadsticks   VEG
Striped Tiger Bites   GF / V (if made with vegan chocolate) / VEG
Iago's Crunchy Seed Clusters   DF / GF / VEG

Beverages

Night Howler Lemonade   DF / GF / V / VEG
Blueberry Sparkler   DF / GF / V / VEG
Sour Bill's Citrus Float   DF / GF / V / VEG
Savanna Sunset Slushie   DF / GF / V / VEG
Witch's Brew   DF / GF / V (if honey is omitted or replaced with maple syrup) / VEG
Chocolate Mud Puddle   DF (if made with nondairy milk) / GF / VEG (if marshmallows are substituted with vegan marshmallows)

Sweets

Chocolate Top Hats   VEG (if marshmallows are substituted with a vegan alternative)
Flame Meringue Pops   DF / VEG
***Sugar Rush* Castle Cupcakes**   VEG
Black Cat Doughnuts   VEG
Elephant Ears   V (if butter and puff pastry are vegan options) / VEG
Treasure Trove Coconut Ice Cream   GF / VEG
Magic Mirror Sugar Cookies   VEG
Captain Hook Brownie Bites   VEG
Maleficent's Triple Chocolate Sandwich Cookies   VEG
Cruella Cookies   VEG
Edible Roses   GF / VEG

Glossary

A

Andouille sausage—a type of smoked sausage, made of pork

Apple cider vinegar—a type of vinegar made from apple juice

B

Baguette—a long, narrow loaf of French bread with a crisp crust

Bake—to cook ingredients in an oven using indirect heat around the food. Many ovens must first be set to a bake setting before the temperature is adjusted.

Baking sheet—a flat metal pan used for baking, especially for sweets like cookies, biscuits, or breads

Blend—to combine two or more ingredients into a smooth mixture

Broil—to cook ingredients using direct heat over the food. Most ovens have broil settings.

C

Candy melts—colored candy chips that are melted and used for baking and decorating

Challah bread—a braided bread of Ashkenazi Jewish origin that is made with eggs, flour, sugar, yeast, and water

Chives—a green, grasslike herb with a mild onion flavor. It's often used as a garnish.

Chop—to cut an ingredient into pieces that are roughly the same size

Chorizo—a type of sausage made of pork

Cloves (garlic)—each segment of a garlic plant bulb

Cloves (spice)—made from the dried flower buds of a tropical tree

Coarse sugar—a large crystal sugar mainly used as a topping on baked goods

Coconut aminos—a salty, dark brown condiment made from coconut sap

Confectioners' sugar—a finely ground form of sugar, also known as powdered sugar

Cream of tartar—a dry powder often used in baking

Creole seasoning—a blend of zesty herbs and spices often used to cook traditional New Orleans dishes

Crumbled—broken or rubbed into small pieces

Cumin—a spice made from the seeds of an herb in the parsley family

D

Dice—to cut foods into small cubes (typically ¼ inch wide)

Dill—a sweet, delicate, green herb harvested from the flowering tops of dill plants

Dragon fruit—a sweet, tropical fruit with a bright magenta- or golden-colored skin and seedy, white or bright pink flesh.

Drizzle—to slowly pour a thin stream of liquid or a melted ingredient over another food

Dust—to lightly sprinkle a powdery ingredient, such as confectioners' sugar or flour. Rolling pins are often dusted with flour to keep them from sticking to piecrust, cookie dough, or other foods that are rolled out.

E

Edamame—a type of soybean that is especially popular in East Asian cuisines

Extract—a concentrated flavoring made by soaking certain foods, such as vanilla beans, in water or other liquids

F

Feta—a crumbly, white cheese of Greek origin most often made of sheep or goat's milk

Fold—to gently blend ingredients by using a spatula to cut through the center of the mixture and then flip one half over the other. Stiff-beaten egg whites are often folded, rather than stirred, into cake and soufflé recipes to keep as much air in the batter as possible.

G

Garam masala—a spice blend widely used in Indian cuisines

Garnish—to decorate a prepared recipe with an herb, a fruit, or another edible ingredient that adds color and/or texture

Grate—to shred foods, such as coconut, carrots, cheese, or chocolate, into bits or flakes by rubbing them against a grater

Ground—when a dry ingredient has been broken up into very small pieces, often with a powderlike texture

H

Herbes de Provence—a blend of dried herbs that is commonly used in French and Mediterranean cooking

J

Jordan almonds—a toasted almond that is coated with a hard, colored sugar shell

K

Kitchen shears—scissors made specifically for cutting food

Knead—to repeatedly fold and press together dough until it is smooth and stretchy. Kneading traps air bubbles produced by the yeast, which is what makes the dough rise.

M

Marinate—to soak food in a flavored liquid for an extended period of time so that the food absorbs the flavor before cooking. The flavored liquid is called a marinade.

Meringue—a type of dessert traditionally made with whipped egg whites and sugar

Mince—to chop ingredients, such as garlic cloves, gingerroot, or fresh herbs, extra fine. This evenly distributes the flavor in the dish you are cooking.

Muffuletta—a type of sandwich originated by Italian Americans in New Orleans

N

Nori—thin sheets of dried, mildly sweet seaweed, mainly used in Japanese cuisine as a food wrap for sushi

Nutmeg—a spice made from the seed of a tropical tree

O

Oregano—an herb commonly used in Mediterranean cuisines

P

Paprika—a spice made from ground dried bell or chili peppers

Parchment paper—heat-resistant paper used to line a baking sheet so cookies and other foods won't stick to the pan when you bake them

Parfait—a layered dessert usually featuring a soft, sweet ingredient (like whipped cream, custard, or ice cream), and fruit that's served in a tall, narrow glass

Pastry tamper—a tool used to press dough into tart or pie pans so that it's even

Pat—to gently tap dough with the palm of your hand

Pepitas—a kind of pumpkin seed commonly used in Mexican cooking

Persian cucumbers—a type of mini cucumber that is narrow and seedless

Pinch—a small amount of a dry ingredient, such as salt or a ground spice, added to a recipe with your fingertips

Piping bag—a cone-shaped bag with a pointed end used to dispense batter, frosting, or other soft food mixtures. To use one, snip the pointed end of the bag and fit a piping tip inside. Fill the bag with your chosen frosting or topping, then twist the open end to seal the bag. Pipe the mixture by pushing it from the sealed end.

Produce—fresh fruits and/or vegetables

Puff pastry—a light, flaky pastry made by combining thin layers of butter and dough

Puree—to blend food until it is completely smooth

R

Rice vinegar—a vinegar made from fermented rice wine. Popular in China, this type of vinegar has a much sweeter taste than Western vinegars

S

Saucepan—a high-sided pan, usually with a handle, and meant for cooking foods on a stovetop

Scallion— a long, green onion with a small bulb on its end

Seltzer water—water that has been combined with carbon dioxide to make it bubbly

Separate egg whites—to divide egg whites (the clear portion of the egg) from their yolks (the yellow portion). To do it, crack the egg and pour its contents into one of the shell halves. Working over a bowl, tip the yolk back and forth into each shell half, letting the white fall into the bowl. Slide the yolk into a separate bowl.

Serrated knife—a small utensil used to delicately peel or cut fruits and vegetables

Shallot—a purple-skinned, bulb-shaped onion with a mild flavor

Shred—to pull or cut an ingredient into many thin strips

Simmer—to cook food on the stovetop in liquid heated just to the point at which small bubbles rise to the surface

Skillet—a flat-bottomed, shallow pan with a long handle used for cooking on a stovetop

Snip—to use kitchen scissors to cut an ingredient into small pieces

Soften—to warm an ingredient such as butter (either by setting it out at room temperature or heating it in a microwave) until it is easy to combine with a mixture

Star anise—a star-shaped, licorice-flavored fruit that is dried and used as a spice. It is used in many Asian cuisines.

Star fruit—a yellow, sweet, tangy tropical fruit that has a distinctive star shape

Steep—to soak an ingredient in water or another liquid to infuse the liquid with the ingredient's flavor

Strain—to remove liquid from an ingredient or mixture by pouring it into a colander, metal sieve, or cheesecloth. The solids are trapped in the colander, sieve, or cloth and liquid drains away.

Sweetened condensed milk—milk that is blended with sugar and simmered until half or more of the water of its water has evaporated. The remaining liquid is thick and creamy.

T

Toss—to mix solid ingredients by gently combining them

To taste—to add just enough of a certain ingredient, typically one or more spices, to improve the flavor of a dish

Turmeric—a brightly colored golden spice made from a root in the ginger family

W

Whip—to beat air into an ingredient, such as cream or egg whites, until the ingredient is light and fluffy

Whisk—a long-handled kitchen utensil with a series of wire or plastic loops at the end used to rapidly beat eggs, cream, or other liquids. *Whisk* is also a verb that means "to use a whisk."

White pepper—a spice made from the dried fruit of the pepper plant. It is more mild than black pepper.

Z

Zest—a flavorful ingredient created from the outermost rind (or peel) of citrus fruits like lemons, limes, and oranges. To zest a citrus fruit, ask an adult for help to find the right kitchen tool, like a zester or rasp grater. Hold the fruit over a bowl and use the zester or grater to gently scrape the outer peel, stopping when you reach the white part of the peel.

Index

Page numbers in *italics* are pictures.